VENUS RISING

LAURA BURKHART

For Shar & Redwan,
precious friends, with
fond memories &
anticipation of many
more adventures!

Love,
Laura

HAGIOS PRESS

Library and Archives Canada
Cataloguing in Publication

Burkhart, Laura, 1952-
Venus rising / Laura Burkhart.

Poems.
ISBN 0-9735567-2-2

I. Title.

PS8603.U75V46 2004 C811'.6 C2004-904230-0

Printed and bound in Canada

The publishers gratefully acknowledge the assistance of the Saskatchewan Arts Board and the Canada Council for the Arts in the publication of this book.

HAGIOS PRESS
Box 33024 Cathedral PO
Regina SK S4T 7X2

For Naomi, Chris, and Kate

CONTENTS

ALL OUR RELATIONS

PILOT PROJECTS

OFF THE TOURIST PATH

WATERMARKS

We live in a rainbow of chaos.
– Paul Cézanne

ALL OUR RELATIONS

SIXTH GRADE SUMMER

The foghorn bellows, a bull moose that strikes
the evening fire to steep the tea. Peppermint stings
my nostrils, stabs my one clear eye, burns an epigraph
into the roof of my mouth: *I can hear it growing*.

Its leaves scratch my hands, carve welts that taste
of lemon. The foghorn didn't really bellow –
the siren blew at noon and six, notice
to put the kettle on, gather chamomile to mix

with peppermint (the leaves will inter-marry and bear
silent children). That summer in Hinton, pulp mill fog
clouded the game of detective I played with Chris,
a kerchief over my nose and mouth, scant protection

from the foul reek. *I smell the mill, man*. We don't
have a mailman. Wrinkled letters wait at the post office
wrapped in onionskin. We scramble
through the valley, boisterous as tiger lilies, sneak

beneath the stream to find our way back. Penny watches
from the tallest foothill, her hand in her mouth. We know
this summer will turn into leaves that burn the morning
orange, the hillside lilies drop their petals

on the count of three, a symphony of nakedness. Still,
we're thick with longing, mouths wide open, bodies poised
to burst, filled with tea and sirens that incant a summer
dance. Fire boils around the pot, spilling from our skin.

VISIT FROM A CHILDHOOD FRIEND

You give my daughter the mystery
I gave you when you turned thirteen:
Nancy Drew, my writing on the flyleaf
uncertain which way to slant. We could

have been ballerinas, such *pointe*
we danced around your father. Nine-year-olds
huddled under goose down in the attic
that enclosed our clouds of breath,
hoping your dad would stay

passed out so we could listen to ships
call each other on his short-wave.
Sneaking to the kitchen summer nights,
naked thieves, we mimed his silence,
danced with chocolate-syruped ice cream
in light cast by the street lamp. Now

we tiptoe around each other,
speak of recycling old newspapers.
You tell me liquid paper will mask
the scratches in my kitchen linoleum.
We're too old, not foolish
enough, to recall ballerina days.

HOUSES

1

At first I don't recognize it. In the soil
I mucked in as a child, nasturtiums grow,
stuccoed walls now festooned with vines,
no gaping doors, no shattered windows.

I follow my ghost footprints,
small and unsure, stand
at the back step, raise my hand to knock,
then see that small girl in cotton print

pyjamas looking from the kitchen window
at the August night. She hears
the crickets, drunken laughter. She sees
her father watching her. His leer

at the neighbour lady turns
to a scowl. He comes inside, hisses
she's supposed to be sleeping, not spying

on a grown-up party, takes her back
to bed, makes sure she stays there,
camouflaged by the sounds of the party
such a few feet away.
Pyjamas torn and sticky
when he tucks her in,

she remembers that her mommy told her
always turn out the light behind you
when you're looking at the dark
too late.

2

I hate houses with flat roofs. My friend
Christine and her five brothers
woke one morning, father gone

mother and the baby inside her
dead, fourteen blows to her belly.

On the porch next to the empty
milk bottles Chris found a note:
Don't wake the children.

That afternoon mothers whispered
in the yard, smoked too many cigarettes,
then scurried to put supper on the table
when the men came home.

3

The house I loved most
had a third story for my children.

So much space, the first night
we moved from our micro-house,

one by one they brought their pillows
to sleep with me, their rooms too large,

too empty. Even there,
for nearly a year I slept

with a chair propped under the doorknob,
until the memories of shadows

against the hallway light
came sharp and clear,

named, screamed,
and gone.

4

If I walked by a flat-roofed house
thirty years later, and saw Christine
looking out the window, would I

recognize her golden hair curled
flat against her head? She looked like the angels
in the picture on my six-year-old

bedroom wall where Mary's being drawn
to heaven like into a vacuum cleaner, her eyes
astounded. Would Christine know me

without my thick glasses? Would she
invite me into her flat-roofed house,
show me pictures of her children,

grown up and gone, pour mint tea
into Royal Albert china cups?
And would we confess the lies

we tell our grandchildren
when they ask about our daddies?

FIFTY WAYS TO LEAVE

Last summer of the century,
a Dylan/Simon concert, Nashville,
open-air arena, a country

song all whine and steel guitar –
I found my adolescence
lost since 1969: Dylan banging

tambourines, harmonica bluesing
through the chorus. A fall kept me
in traction that July, chain-smoking,

watchful lest my father snare me
helpless, morphined in the hospital,
not knowing why *Fifty Ways to Leave*

Your Lover only made me dread
his visits more, early morning,
late at night, the nurses silent at their posts.

At the concert Kevin told me I would scream:
"Some thirty-year-old lyric will touch
your teenage heart."

Soft night against my skin,
strobes kissing 10,000 fans,
my cries were not pure delight.

BALLERINA LAMP

> I am the least difficult of men. All I want
> is boundless love.
>
> – Frank O'Hara

1. The lamp

See that girl by the table lamps? The one fingering her beaded change purse, trying to decide between the ballerina and the shade with plastic cascading flowers? She's saved up her allowance, twenty-five cents a week, to buy this present for her mom. The girl peers through thick-lensed glasses, caresses the silken lampshades. Her fingernails are bitten to the blood line. She would like to sit on a swivel stool at the counter, order an egg salad sandwich and Orange Crush, like when Aunt Sadie brings her here some Saturday mornings. Instead, she takes the ballerina lamp to the check-out, counts out her quarters. The lamp will match her mom's eyes, crinkled dark as a summer sky before a thunderstorm. Her room will look full of love, like the dressing room of a famous dancer, with this glamorous lamp reflected in the mirror on the dresser.

2. The ballerina

The mom stays in bed too late to make the girl's school lunch. The little sister cries and cries in the night so the girl stumbles from her room and takes her to lay beside her, where she leaves a damp diaper stain on the sheet. Sometimes on Saturday nights after the girl has polished the shoes for Sunday Mass and lined them up on newspaper against the kitchen wall, the mother wraps the girl's freshly-washed curls in rags.

When she's done, the girl twirls around the kitchen, arms outstretched. Ringlets fly out from her head, reach straight toward the walls. The little sister giggles from the floor.

3. The lamp

The dad lurches in one night and knocks it off the dresser when he falls against it. The ballerina breaks her leg.

4. The ballerina

When the mom gets old she'll want to wash her hair with lumpy oatmeal. On warm Friday afternoons she'll sit in the park and give advice to hot air balloons that dance away through the splintered sky.

PLAYING DEVIL

My mother stabbed a pitchfork
through her foot and had to bribe
her brother with her favourite book
to feed the cows and keep

her secret. By suppertime her foot
had swollen like the goose she stuffed
for Sunday dinner so she hobbled down
the stairs, confessed her crime.

Before grandma called
the doctor, she called my mother
nasty names, and spanked her
for playing devil in the hayloft.

SATURDAYS, 1959

My mother kept this secret, even from herself: what
went on those summer afternoons she left
us with Dad while she shopped the OK
Economy, brought home Eat-Mores, Kit Kats,
as a special treat.

The first surprise: my brother
learned to walk while she was gone, staggered
to her grocery bags, threw up beer on her shoes.

When we could talk, we begged to come along,
help push the cart, lift Cheerios
from the shelves. But always there were babies
home to watch, in case Dad fell asleep.

One day my sister thought she heard him
snore beneath our bed; either that
or a tramp, she said, jumped off the rails
and snuck in through the basement window.

I took the broom, lifted pink chenille, poured
the flashlight's gleam into the dust.
It was the dog, sleeping, our father upstairs
with our smallest sister, bedroom door closed
and locked.

Later, my mother would cook hot dogs
while we watched Bugs Bunny outwit
Elmer Fudd, our father laughing in his chair.

When Dad choked on cigarettes, turned red, we held
our breath, crossed our fingers, listened
for the wieners boiling on the stove until they burst.

NOVEMBER 22, 1963

Miss Karchinski stopped the lesson,
        participles, gerunds, predicate clauses
brought in the radio, tears blotching
her large Ukrainian bosom
        to match the splotches under her arms.

The President had been shot
in a town I never heard of, the President
of that country I had to memorize:
        mark the capitals on this map; colour
        green for mining, red for manufacturing;
        make sure the rivers all flow blue –
        test on Friday after spelling.

We watch Miss Karchinski blow
her nose in a red dotted hankie, stuff it
in the sleeve of her print dress and turn
the volume up. Sirens and screams,
        there are a million stories in The Naked City
the announcer breaks off, *I can't*
tell you any more. They've taken him
inside the hospital now. The first
lady's dress is covered with blood.

        When my nose bled my mom used my shirt
        as a floor rag, too much blood to bleach.

I hear the teachers crying in the hall,
my friend Joanna, too, although
I know she never knew this man.

David and Alvena,
        sitting in a tree, k-I-s-s-I-n-g
stop passing notes to sit with open mouths.

I had my birthday the day before:
a cake, nine candles, present of a pogo stick,
        green, even the rubber part. I practiced
        in the basement, cement floor hard and cold
        on my bum when I fell
a kiss from my mom and a skinny hug

and now the President is dead
so no one at school will remember
to ask me what I got.

REMNANT

No one but me would look
twice at you in that skirt.
Exhausted blue, it looks sewn

from a remnant my mother might have grabbed
one day when she was half-cut
and lurched into the fabric

shop by mistake on her way to the liquor
store, then whipped up a little straight-
line number for me to wear

to school. Once for my birthday
she sewed a pant suit. She cut
the luscious corduroy I picked out

against the nap, then refilled
her glass so she wouldn't see
the flaw. Looking like a clown

in wavy stripes, I said I'd wear
it anyway (I couldn't stand to see her
cry), wore it once to church

then scrunched it in my closet, piled
other promises on top. You walk
ahead of me, schoolgirl skirt not even

humming in the breeze. You're going nowhere
interesting, if that skirt is any clue. I'm glad
I'm no longer you.

ALL OUR RELATIONS

What happens to remembrances we hold,
those memories we carry in our cells?
All our relations scramble in our minds,
push forth their own translations of the truth.

Those memories we carry in our cells –
grandmothers we may have never met –
push forth their own translations of the truth
and colour how we see the present world.

The grandmother I never met demands
I tell her story, detail every piece:
it colours how I see the present world.
My daughter writes a play of child abuse,

details my mother's childhood, piece by piece,
although she can't have known her silent fear.
My mother asks me how she wrote the play.
I tell her we all clamour to be heard:

alive or dead, we seize the pen at hand,
transform remembrances we hold,
and bring forth versions of truth
whose relations scramble in our minds.

SMALL ROOM, 1971

Rent: ninety hours of work
for a single bed, two-burner stove,
scarred wooden table with one chair, a sink
that sometimes drained. It was larger
than the room I left at home
across from my father's,
the hallway always much too narrow.
For this room I had a lock and key.

I shared the bath with other tenants
who kept secrets from themselves,
scrubbed it before I used it.

I'd grip the filthy phone outside the entrance,
listen to my mother read newspaper
crinkled like her voice. Murders, rapes,
drug deals gone bad – all on the same
block as the house that surrounded
my small room. My mother said
novenas for the safety of my soul.

That summer I was a Woolworth's waitress,
one-fifty an hour and sometimes tips. I paid
the first month's rent and bought
a jar of peanut butter with what was left.

The first night I returned to find
a full ripe watermelon perched
on the burned arborite counter.
Can you blame me for marrying the boy
who brought me such a gift?

AFTER YOUR SISTER'S FUNERAL

Driving from the cemetery, I notice
the tattered sign on the school house, abandoned
long before I lived here. I want to follow
this road past the post office, to the land

we called Over North, check the trap line,
search for ripening saskatoons. Instead
I turn in at the farm and remember us
wrestling with the wind to close

the barbed wire gate, urging the truck through mud,
chasing cattle from the garden. Machine parts
still litter the yard; the gas tank's posted sentinel
by the Quonset, burning barrel

overgrown with brome grass. Now Chelsea
barks as each car and truck arrives
to fill those spaces left by long winter
afternoons with snow pristine and silent

in the yard, all driven by old friends
of ours, here to celebrate your sister
with their sorrow. When I speak Chelsea follows me,
a moan deep in her throat. After all these years

she still thinks she's my dog. The house has spread
into the yard. Russian olive's been replaced
by the back porch you'd always promised me,
as big now as my old kitchen. Even

the wood stove has moved with the walls,
one of them adorned with our daughter's drawing
of three women facing east. Some things haven't changed:
those cupboards in the stairwell bring to mind

your crazy eyes that August night I feared
your rage would push me down the stairs.
You show me your new bedroom – cathedral ceiling,
windows facing west and south. Your new wife

has placed dried flowers on the bedside table.
From the other room I hear our friends
talking of your sister, and I recall
hot summer days she used to visit. We'd watch

our children swimming in the pond, trade recipes
for chokecherry wine. Your new wife looks a bit
like her. I have to get some air. I go outside,
wander through the garden, overgrown with weeds,

tangled raspberry canes, last year's windfall
apples underneath the trees, and want to smoke
back the tears that rise when I slip through
the shelterbelt, recognize the tree that's grown

so much since that summer afternoon you stopped
my weeding and we made love
beneath its fledgling branches. I see the deer
still winter on the apricots you planted,

bushes stunted now, and you've allowed
my asparagus bed to turn back to prairie.
I touch the corpses of strawberries
you gave me, ninety plants, incentive

not to leave. And now your sister's gone, too.
Back in the sparkling kitchen, I watch
you pour home-made wine, red and white,
into plastic tumblers and pass them to the mourners.

MY SON COMES OUT

When Charlene comes in the door I flap
my rubber glove at her, then return
to scrubbing residue of raisin
pie and lima-bean surprise from the oven floor.
I know she'll come in anyway, drop

some garden peppers on the table,
light a Matinée, and blow
smoke rings at the ceiling. I don't need to look
to see her blond bouffant Friday-do
bob up and down as she pokes the cigarette

like exclamation points in her announcement:
"Saw Matthew at the pool again." My arm
continues scouring, turbo-charged piston
pounding at the grime. "He was flirting
with the lifeguard, the body-builder

from the Y." That Charlene would skin
a cat for laughs. I sit back on my heels,
rinse my rag. "It's no affair
of mine," I tell her, stick my head
back in the oven.

IN FRONT OF HER

a grey plane noses through the sky.
Water drips in the lagoon, the grass
beside it echoes the green of his eyes the day
they first made love. Now his shirt,
left overnight on the patio, lies
wet and limp against the wicker chair.

Windows fogged inside with heat, flowers
release their life into the water glass:
white daisies (fickleness), green carnations,
one delicate rose lily bought for his birthday
only one day late.
What else? Laptop computer closed

and silent, two cameras (one for each
perception), zebras from the zoo, sand
dunes, piles of paper, books:
Theory and Numerical Modeling
of Turbulent Gas-Particle Flows
and *Soul Mates* (neither one hers); a half-empty

box of Belgian chocolates, his
blank journal (another birthday gift),
an ad for the Grand Opening
of Legoland in San Diego. She watches
a girl dart past the lagoon and run
out of sight into the rain,
to someplace she's never been.

HIS LETTER FROM PARADISE POINT

Yesterday three thousand tons of sewage
soiled the seals in the bay, perhaps enough
chaos to rouse your rage and spoil our holiday
if you were here. This afternoon

I was wined by eager Japanese
who want to be like me, an old fart
who pontificates in a sweater
with poorly-mended moth holes. Their goal:

to leave their suits and ties at home.
The woman I'm with said you wouldn't mend
the sweater holes because you didn't love me.
Yesterday we found a small café

on the beach where seals siesta
at midday (you'd say I drank too much
Tuscan wine). She said I talk excessively
of you. Perhaps she's still hurt

I went back one last time. I know you
don't care about this, but she will leave me
like you did, even though she claims today
she'll mend my sweater

and write her congressman about the seals.
She makes me wear a condom. I know
she wonders who I write this to.
Still, I am very happy here.

ISRAEL AFTER DARK

1

You learned in hiding when you were young
not to reveal your father's suffering in the war.
Your true name remained unsung.

Your mother's rage against you stung;
its silence shored up the heavy door
that kept back the secrets. When you were young

you designed weapons for Israel's sons
to keep the Chosen safe, to help them soar.
Your true name would never pass your tongue,

not even in dark dreams, those nights you clung
to me, blamed your tears on wine, nothing more.
You learned to keep secrets when you were young,

locked like your silent lovers whose pictures hung
on the shadows of the secrets that you bore:
in hiding, your true name could never pass your tongue.

On Sunday mornings, glasses spilled that once had rung
with empty victories, the spoils of your private war.
You learned to keep secrets when you were young.
Your true name would never pass your tongue.

2

It doesn't matter, I pretend:
one name's good as another.
My parents' secrets I defend.

You hold your own secrets.
I pretend the nights you spend
with other lovers don't matter.

The arms I built to offend
the Chosen's foes, protect my father:
his camp secrets I defend.

When nightmares wake you, I tell
myself to ignore them. They cannot
hurt our life together.

Our silence like the rageful end
of Sabbath meals with my mother:
my parents' secrets I defend.

Silent secrets tear apart our marriage.
We carve each other.
It doesn't matter, I pretend.
Our own secrets, we defend.

ON BEING DUMPED

Petrarch devised a poem to carry grief
and wrote six hundred of the well-shaped rhymes
to Laura whom he met when he was nine.
Five years later the plague claimed her. Their brief
encounters never involved words. Once he
touched her hem. He pined for her all his life.
She never knew how he neglected wives
to pen her sonnets: form that holds barely
spoken love. In Afghanistan you craved
an ice-cold beer. Once at home you forgot
that wanting. In your daydreams you crafted
sculptures of us both. What if I had saved
myself for you? Would you want me or not?
I ask because today my lover left.

NEUTRON

"Don't laugh when I say *neutron*."
Your face was not yet creased
by a wife and daughters, nor the cancer

that would leave your last novel
unfinished. We were young, foolish
enough to stammer of love. I hoarded

your letters, fat with extra postage,
in a birch-bark basket from my grandmother
till one day in a superstitious race

to salvage my marriage, I slipped
them page by page into the fire, watched
the flames transmute your words to ash. That spring

you sailed in unannounced. Pleading *neutron*
erased the years and we were back
in the laundry room, dryer humming a refrain

to your guitar. You sang "Catch the Wind"
but I wouldn't let you catch
my eye, turned my cheek to your kiss.

If I'd gone with you then
I'd be a widow now. I'd have cursed you
when you shipped out for six months

to stevedore those Arctic ships, earn
enough to write the other six while I curbed
the children's noise and late at night

typed your manuscripts while you communed
with your great grandfather
through an Irish whiskey haze.

I would have held your head
when you vomited after chemo,
and fielded phone calls from distant friends,

one of them someone like me, calling
much too late.

RAINBOW OF CHAOS

1. Red

Ani DiFranco belts out rage. Her arms
pretzel around thin legs on the poster
in my daughter's room, my quiet daughter,
well-behaved and serious, no keggers
for her, no biker boy friends, not even
a cigarette behind the gym on a sunny
April afternoon. The dress she wore
to her cousin's wedding bloomed red
against her skin; she found it
at the Salvation Army thrift store,
shield over the entrance
proclaiming salvation.

2. Orange

Children doze in the back seat; sticky arms and legs
sweat against vinyl. This desert is relentless,
sleep the only respite from words, hollow or harsh,
flung from the driver and his passenger wife: smoke
clouds the air. The youngest wakes, vomits on her shirt,
shifts against her brother, then sleeps again
inhaling sour smell, exhaled tobacco.

Windows closed against the shimmer
of heated sand, they drive through scrub, pass
a Texaco. Its flag droops from a wooden pole.
One young girl with large black eyes watches
from the pump, scuffs her bare feet in the dust.
The Rambler lifts a cloud as it passes.

The tarnished sunset spits upon the dunes,
ochre flame across sienna haze.

3. Yellow

Lellow my daughter would brag,
pointing to her hair, those wispy tendrils
like dandelion-fluff,
delicate as her gap-toothed smile.

My colour-blind son could never have
too many yellow clothes. I wonder
what hues he saw, mix and matching
shades from gold to taupe.

Melted butter on popcorn. Painted Easter eggs.
A Volkswagen Beetle. Lemonade stand
on the corner, children drinking
their profits in the hazy afternoon.

Kitchen walls too bright those summer
mornings after fights that kept
us breathless through the night –
a mocking sunlight.

4. Green

I sit in an empty sand box
beside a trailer, listen to my mother
scream because I can't stop coughing.
Three little sisters cower in the back
seat of a faded emerald Rambler, play
with empty whiskey bottles. The garden's
over-run with weeds and cigarette butts.

The colour of envy, although I read once
to beware a man who isn't jealous –
it means he's emotionally bankrupt.
An apt description of a certain rake

I used to love who now – who knows? –
may be painting green swastikas
on his neighbour's fence late at night
while errant children sneak into his garden
and slash his cabbages.

Decades later (my own children grown
and gone) you and I passed by the camel
at the Cairo auction. Still it followed us,
stood sentinel beside the algae-coloured Nile
that night we never touched, but swallowed
words and sighs, returned to separate rooms
whose pale green walls reflected sleeplessness.

5. Blue

Mrs. Stewart's Liquid Blueing keeps
diapers white. Or you can hang them
in the morning sun. When my son was three
he chased a ball into the street. It's true.
My body so heavy on the sofa
I couldn't move until the screeching
tires pulled me to the door.

Fifteen years later we drove
the back hills of Kentucky
past cotton and tobacco fields
on roads that wound like wool unravelled
through pesticidal clouds that blocked the sky.
At a Brownsville diner the waitress
slapped blue willow plates of deep-fried catfish
on Formica tables and called us *Honey*
while an old woman with a washboard
belted out *Muleskinner Blues.*

6. *Indigo*

ink, indigo ink, makes you stink. It spills
from the well on your desk. Seamus
bumped it running by and now your dress
is splattered, bright splotches
on the flowered poplin (your mom
won't sew you another), like globs of mud
on the hopscotch game
when the school bus splashes by.

Your mom will tell you
to wear it anyway, wash it separately
so the ink doesn't bleed on the other clothes.
You'll refuse, will crush it to the back
of your drawer, wear your other dress instead
until it smells of gym class. Then you'll know
it's true: *indigo ink makes you stink,* and Seamus
will hold his nose as he lopes past your desk,
will never notice that the ink matched your eyes.

7. Violet

She smells of lavender, pansies, violets,
scents to match her name. *Always sit*
with your back to the wall facing the door,
she tells me, *so you can keep an eye*
on who is coming and going.

Her world used to be big as the pasture
full of wild horses, grew to include
the atlas maps, library books and silent
pictures (Mary Pickford, Buster Keaton),
the fragrances in Woolworth's, dreams
of New York streets – then to one

small farmhouse, seven children,
a man who seldom washed his hands,
and now this room – a bed, a chair, small dresser
with a silver brush and mirror, a doorway
view of a hall with lilac walls, a granddaughter
who rarely comes to visit.

SCRABBLE

Before he lost his language
and could only scowl and gesture
we used to play this game. He would sulk
if I took the space he wanted. He thought
I should let him win. That's what daughters
did back then. The same way I had learned
to bite my nails and swallow
fear like water, I offered openings
like prayers.

My daughter and I choose our tiles.
She looks through me. "You won't
like this," she says, "but you look
like your father." My gut contracts.
I cannot stretch my stubborn word
to a double letter score. "It's your eyes," she says.
These eyes that don't see as they once did.
And she with perfect vision.

My daughter turns my *rid* to *meridian* on the
triple word score. Of course she wins the game:
unafraid, she gives no charity. Her eyes
focus on each letter, each new word.

PILOT PROJECTS

DESERT CONTRA AND OTHER STORMS

blinding light hot sand insects jump
rusting tanks fill with dreams of young men
campesinos huddle behind trees to watch
young boys in camouflage trudge past
wide-mouthed screams
reporters yell into cameras
soft waves lap over submarines
electrical towers topple
silent in the jungle heat
AK-47s nest against trees
women kiss the blood-tongued flowers they pass

DATELINE MOZAMBIQUE

1. Grandpa Pedro

Climb this mango tree, Sophia Pedro.
You'll have a good view of the killer
waters, watch them eat our maize crop, now
washing brown with baked dirt you hoed, sun
burning, belly heavy with your baby. Here,
let me boost you up, grab that branch,
careful now. Take this blanket, only
a little damp. Can you hear the waters
from up there, see those folks stranded
on the bridge? Better climb a little
higher, just in case the water's hungry.

2. Sophia Pedro

The night she be long, the air so damp
from water raging. Who else be in this tree?
Mama Lucie, that you there behind that branch?
This baby, she be wanting to come see
'bout all this fuss. She paining me
real good, my belly getting hard. And now
my own water added to floods below.
What's all that yelling? That be me?
Or ghosts living in this mango tree
screaming out my pain? OK I hear you
Mama Lucie. I take the blanket,
stretch it tight across the branches. I have
no hat for this child when she born.
Tell me what to do.

3. Mama Lucie

You doing fine my child. You rest between
the pains. And when they come bite hard
on mango leaves to give you strength. That noise
you hear is all them folks, cheering
from the bridge, taking bets on boy or girl,
yelling you their favourite names, for such
a tree child will be special, blessed by God.
Your mama will be proud of you, Sophia,
and your no-good husband who went to find
a boat will tell the men this story
of his wife who was so brave. Now bite
down hard, and when that child won't wait no more
just push her out and catch her in the blanket.

4. Sophia Pedro

Rositha, lovely daughter, born unto this water
that rose six metres from sun to sun and set again.
Will you grow so swift, my lovely daughter,
strong as this sad country, hungry from
the journey? And what about the land we lost,
she be gone with water, now only fear
of cholera and famine. Already you growing
to a girl of strength, soon a woman of great courage.
But sleep for now, protected in the mangoes.
The boat may come tomorrow.

5. Rositha

I am the one they call Rositha,
girl born in a tree. They think this gives
me special powers. They will say
it took two months for foreign food
to come, and many people died, while I
grew strong and bright-eyed
on my Mama's meagre breast.

When I grow up my Mama will find
school fees, even though the waters
ate our land. This I know.
The wind and river tell me.

PAMPHLETS FOR THE PILOT PROJECT

(Nile Delta)

What use would it be, to gather goat dung,
dry it in the noon sun that beats down harder
than rain, to build the fire,
skim the film atop my water jug, shoo away flies,
boil this water for the time it takes to walk again
to the drainage canal, refill the jug, hoist it
to my head and walk back, greedy heat sucking
moisture even through the cloth laid over top,
then coming back to find half the water gone,
and the other half not yet clear,
the fire eaten its share of air and ready to sleep
away the afternoon? What use to purify
this water to feed my babies when I see already
the parasites behind their listless eyes?
What use the government pamphlets –
they do not even burn so well to kindle the noon-day
fire, too much coloured ink that makes the babies
cough, disturbs the flies from their nostrils.
What use is it to gather my anger
like sun-bleached laundry from the banks
of the canal, line it up with tanks from the Six
Days War that still litter the ungreened desert?
What use to recall the ones who come
in air-conditioned cars with drivers, who listen
to us women, even let our babies touch their golden rings
then drive away again without drinking our tea,
their briefcases full of papers filled with facts? Later,
they send back a photo of us, dressed in our Friday
best (We hang it in the empty health office), along
with pamphlets filled with pictures that tell us not
to drink the water –

TRAVEL

In a country where my only connection
to home is the answering machine message
at the Canadian embassy (I call it late
at night from my hotel), I walk anonymous
streets and marvel: I could disappear
into an open manhole and no one would know.

In a civilized line I wait to change
currency: dusty light from long slanted windows
speckles the bank's marble floor. Tired of listening
to Spanish conversations, I read an English
paperback, then realize (I'm almost at the front
of the queue) in the final chapter
I've read it years before.

Riding buses packed with people, chickens
tethered to the seats, barely enough air, I
sway in aisles, watch volcanic mountains flash
by filthy windows. I force myself to sleep
so I'll be relaxed, lose fewer limbs
when the lunatic driver tumbles us
over the edge into the valley
of shanty towns.

Back home I hunger for the morning
call to prayer, streets crammed with strangers,
traffic blaring past. I cannot help
my daughter learn her algebra or sleep
past 5 a.m. or rid myself of dreams
that I miss the connecting flight.

ISRAEL'S INFANCY

An interview on CBC with Amos Oz:
Like you, he moved to Israel at its birth
from hiding somewhere else. He learned
to speak Hebrew and how to play
in sun-washed village streets. Every
night the air erupted, nightmare screams
filled with messiahs and dream
messengers that caught morning
dew from water tower steps.

I hear Oz say that when he was a child
he wanted to be a book: *People are so easy*
to kill. If I were a book one copy might
survive. Perhaps to rest on a shelf
in the local library. I shut off the radio,
press your broken past between my pages.

GOOD FRIDAY

(Egypt)

> It was now about the sixth hour and the
> sun's light failed, so that darkness came
> over the whole land until the ninth hour.
> The veil of the Sanctuary was torn right
> down the middle.
>
> – Luke 23:44-45

At six o'clock local time
the darkened desert swirls
in city streets; men wish
for the *chodor* to save
their skin from blasting sand.
Women hide in doorways, fold
children in their skirts.
Wind and dark noises
take over emptied streets.

At six o'clock a sudden hail storm
blocks the sun. Donkeys stop,
listen to the oranges bounce off
their carts into the gutter. Camels turn
to face the wind. Impatient
men at traffic lights shake
their silent cell phones, notice
that the lights are locked on red.

At nine o'clock the sand stops whirling.
Hailstones glisten, melting jewels
against the cobblestone. The veil of sky
peels back. In this luminescence,
spouses disclose infidelities of the heart.

HOW DEEP DOES FRIENDSHIP REACH?

> This is the real world, indifferent,
> unburdened.
>
> – James Galvin

Mount Everest is littered with frozen corpses, those who never made it, left at the side of the trail, impossible to carry down or bury, earth and rock unyielding.

But Everest is far away. We're hiking *Cache La Poudre,* path steep and sharp enough to make me pay attention lest I slip into the gorge, break myself on the partly frozen river, even though up here the air is warm, my flannel shirt too heavy. A Chinook wind blows Nora's words, *I'm starting to hate all Muslims.* I'm in America: all rock and scrub and cloud. Nora stops to drink at an icy stream. I tell her about Amira, my Egyptian colleague, doctorate from Oxford, non-religious Muslim, who just the week before invited me to see her new apartment in old Cairo. She told me, *I hold every North American personally responsible for each child killed in Palestine.* I asked her if she'd poison me at dinner. She told me I'm her friend.

We pass a stone twice as tall as me, on which someone has painted *In God We Trust* beside a US flag. Which God. Yahweh? Allah? Christ? And how long before the stone shrugs off this human desecration?

Nora says *of course we are most powerful, Israel our ally, economic interests to protect,* her voice as sharp as rocks I stumble on, her words assured as the mountain jay perched on that outcrop of quartz, surveying what he thinks is his domain. I ask myself how I, a pacifist, came to choose sides in this war that can't be won. Later, I will tell my lover, "I'm as arrogant as my Alabama friend who thinks God made her country the apex of the world, some heavenly reward for being white and rich and righteous."

Amira apologized for what she called her *Arab passion*. I reassured her, made excuses for democracy gone wrong, told her, "We're not all George Bush." I tell Nora we can disagree and still respect each other, but pick my way more carefully going down the rocky trail.

OFF THE TOURIST PATH

SAUCE FOR THE GOOSE

Blackberry cliffs open the pie-
shaped sky, ripple, whirr, lick the clouds
to wander, syrup and dark
arias bleeding across the ice
cream plains. What's sauce for the
goose is open as pie vents, slits
tearing through the cloth of the family
photo album, rush, swish over
the sea foam. Lighthouse flashes:
Warning! to the gander.

ANOTHER NIGHT

spent watching, in the light of the quarter moon,
a fan push humid air across my body
restless in this bed, its sheets as tangled
as if you were here beside me.

Another night hearing the screech of others
still awake, who, reckless as those
in love, leave rubber on the main drag
half a block from this open window.

Another night listening for the crash, wail of sirens,
picturing the light standard twisted
across the sidewalk in the morning when I
tiptoe by and wonder if you slept.

LIGHTNING AFTERNOON

Her mother, had she known,
would have sought eighteen novenas
from the cloistered celibates
for the saving of her daughter's soul.

The daughter even shocked herself
that afternoon the lightning flashed
across their nakedness.

Her husband in Nice
with his mistress,

she dreamed the man
beside her took two lovers
and she told them of each other,
knowing all the while it was she

he really loved, this darling of the lightning
afternoon, thunder fading in the distant
mountains as she turned

to him again. Deception is so simple
if you don't believe in God,

unless you're the one betrayed.
And she asked him: "Is this revenge?
Or true love at last?"

CAIRO NIGHT

1

"This could be a chapter
in your travel book." We dodge the symphony of horns,
dancing octaves, tuning up for the blast

that propels us across
the darkness broken only by speeding headlights. *Maybe
a short story.* A lightless jitney phantoms past.

It deserves its own poem, built
with the rhythms of this night – heat as golden as his
wedding band rises from pavement dark

as his face, dark as the windows
on the passing military car, its siren shrill. No street lights
gloss the way; only his light shirt casts back

the flaming headlights.
Frenzied drivers pack four lanes into three, break all
traffic laws, hand signals illegible to our English minds.

2

Faces sultry with the night,
sudden silence bristles the space between us. Across my lentil soup I watch him lift grains of rice to his lips.

Remember "The Purple Rose
of Cairo," how the heroine falls in love with the actor? and he steps out of the screen

to live in her fantasy –
or is she living in his? Later, we play chicken with the lights flaring past, pressed by horns through the night.

3

Above the North Atlantic,
Modern Woman defines how to lie: *Your soufflé is delicious; you are the best lover I've ever had.*

When he phones I'll tell him
I am fine; there is no traffic here.

OFF THE TOURIST PATH

When you turned and found me
waiting, you passed your palm
across your eyes, reached out
and touched my cheek. But wait –

that's not how it happened – I never
met you as you'd asked, only to say
good-bye in another airport. No,

that time I was the one to travel.
(You'd volunteered to be my bodyguard,
remember? – expedite my pass
through customs, walk always
on the sidewalk by the traffic. I never
called your bluff.) Months later,

when you phoned to ask if I was happy
with my lover, my *yes*
would not have been a lie
before I heard your voice, remembered

how you carried my computer up
four flights every morning, and returned
at 4:00, hands filled with jasmine,
to invite me for a walk
along the river, noonday heat

a memory. Later, driver weaving
back to the hotel through dusk-laden
squatters searching for their evening meal,
we'd speak of bringing water to the desert,
of holidays in France, and exploring

off the tourist path. You know all this, of course,
but did you know I was thinking
about your hand, relaxed on the seat,
how I wanted to touch your fingertips
so lightly you would think
a breeze had gentled through the air? That time

was just a fantasy, I tell myself:
my lover here is real, asleep beside me.
I know his body better than my own,
while yours I've never touched, save for that
handshake when we said good-bye
in an airport the first of many times.

LETTER FROM THE OTHER WOMAN

> You don't use imagination to dream up
> improbabilities. You use imagination to
> penetrate deeper what you already know.
> – Robertson Davies

I never thought I was that kind of woman
until I met your husband. We were broken
open, driverless cars on a snowy highway.
We called our collision love,
then questioned all the rules of marriage.

Every day I played the whore in my Catholic marriage,
but never planned to be the other woman,
made up rules to keep me safe from love
that didn't fit inside my vows. Now we're both broken.
Ignoring the warning rail, we veered off the highway,

bumped across a minefield we called love
and came to rest against a fence, bruised, broken,
hearing cars speed by on the distant highway.
What if I'd been a more honourable woman,
would you still have a marriage?

I made a rule that bound me to my marriage:
Never speak to another man of love.
He broke that rule I had forgotten
and I suddenly became the other woman.
Those rules that killed my marriage became a high way

to lie, to die, to crash beside a highway,
to watch frozen while you two pretended marriage
could be salvaged with false promises: a woman
and man who told themselves their early love
could sustain them – now all is broken.

TRUTH OR DARE

> What do you plan to do with your one wild
> and precious life?
>
> – Mary Oliver

I told myself you had to lie, protect
the coffin of your life, nail down

the lid through my open hands, so I played
along, pretended you spoke the truth, then wept

in the shower Monday morning, added my small
water to the flood, not wanting to alarm

my daughter, who still believes that mommies
only bandage scraped knees, don't have their own

wounds to seal from the air. "I never really
loved you after all." Was this the highest

form of self-delusion – to think you lied
so I wouldn't feel the truth squeeze

my heart so tight I couldn't breathe?
Perhaps you did not lie. Your life

is self-contained and I don't fit: a slight
distraction blown to fantasy. Dreams –

of conversations, a kiss so real
it woke you in the night, love poems

penciled on the backs of envelopes,
and working in North Africa (pretending

it was OK to pretend to be together) -
these dreams that float through nights

of empty darkness, the steady
breathing of your wife, her rhythm

syncopated with your own – you bolt
upright. It's 3:00 a.m. How can you leave

all that you know for this small
possibility? You still your breath, slip

out of bed, push thoughts of me
away, and read a file you've brought

home from the office over and over,
until the text makes sense. Meanwhile,

my silent phone casts a midnight shadow.
You've told your lie. Now we live it.

QUESTIONS I MAY NOT LIKE THE ANSWERS TO

Do you bite your fingernails at night,
slip them to your mouth when you can't sleep,
when dreams of me wake you, hard
and wanting? Where would we be now

if I'd become pregnant that long night
in Tripoli, "Welcome Mrs.
Your-Last-Name" scrolled upon the hotel
TV screen, the room motif in black and white
reflecting how you saw your world? If I met

you now, two seasons later, would we walk
around the man-made lake that centres
this small city, act like friends,
stop for tea, talk about our work?
If I asked, would you tell the truth:

Do you miss me every day? Do you wonder
if our love would have burned
out like a meteor hitting the atmosphere?
If our togetherness
had been a newborn child,
would we be tender parents?

VALENTINE'S DAY

Early fog shrouds the pyramids.
The orange moulded plastic
chair in the Cairo airport holds
the cold like a silent sentry
guarding the sphinx. I left
behind the pale roses you gave me
(memories are the best gifts, you said
when I asked to take your photo).
I tell myself my tears don't matter,
I'm invisible here, orange plastic
hard against the concrete corner.
I tell myself a heart, blood-hungry
muscle shattered, can find release
under pale fluorescent lights. I'm invisible
as I was to you, the wake-up call
you slept through.

A woman stands beside me, English
stranger, puts her hand on my shoulder,
says, "I feel your pain," says,
"It's not your fault that man
is weak." I weep for our clichés and her
compassion, then notice I am freezing,
cold creeping from the plastic. I'm cold
as your name, as the roses
wilting in the empty hotel room.

ROOM

I'm laying on this narrow sofa
no room for you beside me. Tonight
I have a headache, want only
this yellow woollen blanket.
I'm thinking maybe sex for you
is only anger and revenge

when my daughter calls, worried about
her room-mate's diet – *lose ten pounds*
in seven days – and I'm swept back to her
conception, which actually I don't remember,

only the shock of learning
my menstrual cycle had betrayed me,
changed its pace without my knowledge
or permission, and now nineteen years

later the phone calls me from this narrow
sofa for an hour conversation
with a girl who needs her mom.

Now the night has deepened. Baseboard
heaters creak in protest. The wind
blows gingham curtains on the inside
of the panes and makes eerie chimney music.

I lay beneath the yellow woollen blanket,
muse about you and sex
and the difference between making love
and fucking (we have done both).

I try to finalize some definitions
but it's too late. My headache wants
an aspirin, and I know you will not call.

THIS DREAM IS NOT

I'm driving Jacqui's mini-van, her consolation
prize for staying with a sombre man
and three pre-school girls she fears
will become teenagers. The van is full

of friends and children, much too packed,
like the old Cadbury commercial where the cows
keep on coming from the barn, and you know,
even though you're only eight, they're passing

past the camera more than once. There are no stars.
An avalanche fills the road ahead with snow,
a lob atop the prairie pancake. I swerve
around the first pile, drive too fast

into the dark, hit the next snow bank
head-on. This dream is not about you
or your call from India last night.
The van collapses like a cardboard house.

My friends are angry, won't speak to me.
One says I should have gone around
the snow. I show him the cliff waiting
to demolish us. This dream is not about

the lesser of two evils. My dream children
are still young, one only five, one dandelion-
fluff-headed toddler, one just a shadow.
Jacqui pops the van up, hammers

the dents smooth with her fists. This dream
is not about your marriage. When I leave,
run across the empty fields, none of us know
if I will return.

WATERMARKS

DIALOGUE FOR TWO INTERIOR VOICES

If you'd run that light last Saturday
we could be on the beach right now
with Kerouac and Ginsberg
floating in a whiskey haze, and chuckling
at the accountant you'd become
compelled by hours, numbers, prison
sentences of composition.

Accountants are good, necessary,
and very helpful in arranging
the world you've come to expect:
raw oysters on the half-shell, $16
1992 Dom Perignon, $120
chocolat du Bernard Callebaut, $9
18% tip, another wasted evening
and Kraft Dinner for the rest of the week.

I devour you, spit out the knobs
of your spine like marbles.
I masticate your muscles,
make them soft as sweat against the sun.
I split your skin open, blow light
through your veins, clear your mind
of all debris, sweep the ancient dust
from every cell.
Throw away your clock.

You demand I make as much for you
as any corporate banker. You ask me
to rip away this shroud
and build ice sculptures of nuns in
pirouette, scrape a diamond
across the window pane in a pattern
of a summer noon, and blow fresh
flowers to the children passing by.

Turn off that growling calculator! Lean
into the wind. Name the sky cerulean.
Remember when you ran naked
through the poplars? sprawled on the grass
and allowed the sun to kiss your breasts?

This house demands I fit within its walls
of tactful terra cotta, ignore your muted
music seductive as a pomegranate.

You crave a dance with me
among the stars; we could weave lilies
into reliquaries for tears, read books
in languages we cannot understand,
and cultivate a habit of burning
candles through the day,
counting down the smoky hours.

QUESTIONS FOR HAGOP SANDALDJIAN
(Micro Miniaturist, 1931–1990)

Did you learn the hard way that a sneeze
could dash months of work
under a microscope? What prompted *Little*

Red Riding Hood? How did you grind the rubies
and diamonds into powder, fashion each paint brush
from a strand of hair? (my own would be much

too coarse.) *The Kid in the Eye of the Needle*:
Is that how you felt when you moved from Cairo
to Armenia? When did you learn to work

late at night after trucks stopped raising dust
that filtered through windows, contaminated
the *Grapes in a Needle's Eye*? And look –

there's *Goofy* standing on top of a needle, next to
the one of *Pope John Paul*, his mitre brushing

the top of the eye (my own water, squint through
the lens). Was it yoga or beekeeping or *A Wish*

on a Piece of Hair that taught
the stillness you needed

to paint the next mote
in the space between

heartbeats?

DROUGHT

In the third month with no rain
Jan dropped her housewife role
beside the sink and went back
to school. Ed watered the wasps
clustered on the bathroom window
seeking air-conditioned comfort,
then laid the coil against the wall,
went in to fix a sandwich for their son.

In the fourth month the leaves turned
on the trees, and dripped their parched
orange life on the ground. Only
August and branches bare, corn withered
on the stalk. Jan studied every
evening. Ed built a porch swing
to watch fireflies with their son.

That was the year tobacco burned
in the fields and pebbles rattled
in the dry creek bed.

TOBACCO

When she brushed past, the air of scented lilacs
was taken by her tobacco smell. Not cigarette
smoke that clings to clothes, to hair, fouls
the pew on Sunday mornings, but tobacco,

the clean smell of it heaped on the kitchen table
summer nights: Mom fixing rollies for herself
and Dad, tamping dried leaves in the machine
(not too tight or it won't draw; too loose and it'll burn

too fast, fall off the end, drop embers on his
Sunday suit). Moisten the edge of the long Zig-Zag
paper, slide the roller, cut the long
tube into four with a razor, push the smokes

out and pile them in tobacco cans laying
on their sides. See the perfect circles of dark
haloed with white against the tin. Once I stole a long
one before it was cut, wanted to play fancy

lady, fashioned a holder from tin foil.
The elegance bent when I lit it, broke off,
dusty crumbs spotted the floor. Three cans
filled with cigarettes would last a week, less

time when my sisters and I pilfered some.
We offered to perform the rolling ritual, made
extra for ourselves, hid them in our room, can
squashed between bed and window.

The girl with the tobacco scent who brushed
past me, steps straight, eyes focused
where I can't see, may just have stepped
from a tobacco field in Kentucky. A young man

on his way to a treatment centre where smoking
was banned begged his father to stop so he could roll
in the green leaves, a last gift for his skin that would
soon feel only honeysuckle air. This is also true:

In Nicaragua, still a smoker, I mourned
when Contras burned the only cigarette paper
warehouse. At the co-op farm a man
from Maine rolled me a Drum cigarette –

pure bliss against the backdrop
of pubescent boys on street corners, guarding
the Revolution with M16s. The Sandinista
woman I lived with, a health brigadista, bought

me black market cigarettes. I never asked
for that show of solidarity. Last summer,
my seventh smoke-free, I went back to the farm
of my marriage. In the berry patch, I felt the ghost

of every cigarette I'd inhaled rise up and
goose-step through my blood. Right then,
I would have killed to smoke.

WIDOW'S WORK

Water gushes over
the pail edge, and she fills
the kettle on the stove,
heats it for soup
for another empty day.
Then she'll heat more water,

to wash the clothes he wore
that afternoon he dove
into the creek to save
the drowning calf. Now both
are gone, pulled down
by weeds that tangle legs.
She'll scrub the clothes just like

she washed his body, blue
and torn by roots along
the bank, crushed by forty
years of farming. She'll hang
the clothes out on the line,
watch the sun bleach them dry
as bones, before she milks the cow.

I WONDER WHOSE MADNESS SHE CARRIES

A sister, I carried for thirteen years, till I

exchanged her for a marriage and left her
in a house of silent rage that bloomed

at night in colours much too red;
flowers shook in pallid morning. Some days

I carry her still. We've shifted from parent
-teacher interviews to psych wards

coloured pale, mouth-drying pills
Lithium, Zoloft, Stelazine.

I carried a marriage for thirteen more, three
children, a city job, the farm: five-

gallon pails of wash water up cellar stairs, sacks
of salt to soften water, whispering

baskets of diapers, dreams flapping
in the winter wind. It twisted

my shoulders with its weight, ligaments wound
around each other, encased in Monday

mornings of fresh-churned butter on steaming
bread, newest child scooping compost from the pail

set by the door, dripping left-over breakfast
yolk on the pitted floor freshly waxed and glossy

after Sunday sex. Sometimes my sister
would visit, help me wash the clothes,

feed them through the wringer into rinse tubs
of chapping cold. My arms embraced

the withered marriage, my sister numb and parched.

AT EMMA LAKE

1

After lunch I turn into my cat, Natasha,
curl in the joining of two windows
where the sun argues with itself
how much heat to toss upon my body,
heavy as a night empty of love.

I swim into dreams punctuated
by chattering squirrels, rustling poplars,
waves that kiss the sandy shore.
August heat, bones
too chilled for even it to warm.

When my daughter left, Natasha slept
all day, wouldn't rouse for food
nor play, moved only to follow
the sun. At Emma Lake your absence
fills me, scent of sun through glass.

2

When we met as teens my husband
was astounded I could sit
unmoving for hours
doing nothing.

Today I watched the wind breathe
through the poplars, leaves reflect green
against white drops of light on water.
I remembered that lost art.

3

Late afternoon. I walk along a road
packed down by many years of cars and wagons,
even sleighs. It feels to my bare feet
like the kitchen floor of the house I shared
in Estelí, with Graciela and her Sandinista
children. Each morning while Graciela
pounded corn into tortillas, Reyna scrubbed
the floor (swept the soapy water out the door),
dirt packed from generations
of campesino feet, hard as the scarred linoleum
on this cabin floor, this cabin somewhat
larger than their home, and built

about as well, except these walls boast
no bullet holes. One morning
Paulo and Diego played too rough.
The wall woke me (dreaming
of you, even though we'd not yet met)
when it fell across my bed.

4

That hot-dog spandex-coated water
gymnast turning somersaults outside
the buoys, Norse-god body sparkling
in the fading light – yes,

that one, now skiing by again
making waves that rock my body
(first time in this water, not
a swimmer). I silently applaud

and wonder if he's showing
off for me, can't tell from my
submersion I could stand
in for his mom.

5

This kind of sky they'd call
a fake, if you painted
those garish corals, jades,
turquoise casting
their colours on the lake.
Fingernail moon slips behind

a cloud, white counterpoint
on indigo. The wind is silent
as those coyotes on the hill,
statue-like in appreciation,
or watching for small game
backlit against this necklace night.

6

After a four-minute
conversation, it's time
to call the rehydration squad;

this phone booth is a sauna.
It drips with words unsaid:
cancer, radiation, fear.

In another conversation
the silent words say sorry, thank you,
love, lover, loving, loved, and ex.

BAND-AIDS

I saw three of them yesterday, two crossed in a puddle
like ten year olds' fingers, cross my heart and hope
to die I promise I won't tell now show me the pictures
of naked ladies your dad hides beneath his work bench,

Band-Aids facing up their flesh tones reflect the grey
west coast sky on this bleak prairie day.
The other one

in the park on the path I trudged between the spates
of rush-hour traffic, that no-man's time between
between. This one facing

down, the used part up, a memory of white
now depleted, not even pretending to hold
the cracked earth together.

Today in the noon-hour aquafit class my friend scooped
something from the water, tossed it to the deck not
missing a beat, his rhythm so sure. *What was that*? I asked.
A Band-Aid, he said. *If you knew what they found*
in these filters you'd stay out of the pool. I plugged my ears.
Don't tell me.

OLD MASTERS

On New Year's Eve, the year before
their marriage broke, Sue and Mark
invited me to paint with them. Snow
sleeted outside the picture
window. Mark drew
from photographs and postcards;
Sue from somewhere
deep within her dreams.
I felt the tension in my fingers
as I raised the brush, ran
it through the ivory, watched it breathe
into the church in the village square
where the woman in black (protected

by her shroud from shimmering heat)
carried a jar of turquoise water.
Leaves cast dappled shadows
against adobe walls, bell tower silent
after calling the angelus. Two clouds
hovered over this woman who stopped
to rest on the worn step, then reshaped
themselves, darkened like the night
outside the picture window.

I remembered a girl I used to baby-sit,
whose parents couldn't speak
without tearing apart old injuries. Finally,
she sickened and died. But when Sue and Mark spoke

it was with kindness: old masters at marriage,
led into silence thick and layered
as ancient paint, and a final wrenching
apart as harsh as prying windows
painted shut.

We painted till the morning light revealed
that snow had covered last year's tracks.

The woman in my painting watched
cats gaze through potted flowers from a heightened
window sill, adjusted her shroud,
prepared to lift her water jug and carry on.

VENUS RISING

My vision not as clear
as yours, I couldn't see Venus
rising the summer evening
we drove back from Kananaskis
to the pot of heated herbs

and hot Jacuzzi. Months later, home
from the mountains, you took me
to the valley, rusty crinkled
leaves still dancing on the maples
to the gusty prairie song.

You asked me to surmise a wind
that blew a thousand miles
an hour. I saw the sun obscured
by scudding clouds, the sagebrush torn,
great gouges in the earth where now

two rabbits played. That wind would dredge
iced memories of infidelities
at late-night parties, our costumed bodies
dripping silent rage, wooden limbs pretending

desolation was just a passing breeze, till all
was gone save gaping words in leaden skies
with no one left to hear. We've told ourselves
we're different now, that constancy and tenderness
can be relearned. Don't ask me to remember

such a wind. I pulled my jacket tighter.
You pointed out a deer that loped along
the fence, a speck to me.
We clambered over beaver dams,
traced a stream up the hillside

to its source – that gift you brought
me there to see – a tiny spring
that bubbled from the ground
to feed the maples and the deer. Later,
at a dinner party, telling the story

of the secret spring, I left out the part
where we made love, back-lit
by the fading afternoon,
curious rabbits rustling in the brush
while Venus rose, silent in the sky.

ACKNOWLEDGEMENTS

Some of these poems have been published previously in various issues of *Spring, Transition, Prairie Fire,* and on the Canadian International Development Agency website.

Many thanks for their mentoring support to David Jauss, Natasha Sajé, and Joan Crate.

Thanks also to my mother, brother, and sisters, and to Michael, for their love and encouragement.

Thanks to Grove Press for permission to quote Frank O'Hara's "Meditations in an Emergency" as an epigraph for "Ballerina Lamp," page 15. Thanks also to Mary Oliver for permission to use her words as an epigraph for "Truth or Dare," page 65.

Born in Kitchener, Ontario, the third of six children, Laura Burkhart spent her first six years on various construction sites in northern Alberta before the family moved to Edmonton. In 1967 they moved to Saskatchewan, where Laura lived until her recent move to Hawai'i. She has three grown children, all of whom are active in the arts, and has travelled to Asia, the Middle East, and Latin America as a consultant in international development. She holds an MFA in creative writing from Vermont College.

Venus Rising is set in Palatino Linotype, a typeface designed by Hermann Zapf in 1948 and issued by the Stempel Foundry in Frankfurt, where it was first cut by hand in metal. The self-taught Zapf later adapted the face for the Linotype machine, and with the advent of phototypesetting Palatino became one of the most widely-used typefaces in the world. Palatino Linotype was issued by Linotype, now a digitally based type foundry, in 2000.

Designed and typeset by Donald Ward, who also designed the cover.

Cover photo (detail) by Laura Letinsky, from her book *Venus Inferred*; courtesy of Edwynn Houk Gallery, New York.

Author photo: Karin Whitney Cooke.

Edited by Joan Crate.